thread me an exit

THREAD ME AN EXIT was a winner of the 2024 Brain Mill Press + Wisconsin Fellowship of Poets Chapbook Contest.

thread me an exit

poems

wendy vardaman

Brain Mill Press
Green Bay, Wisconsin

Some of the poems in this collection first appeared in the following publications and are reprinted here with permission:

"piecework" appeared in BlazeVOX Journal.

"piecework" and "postcards from the museum of childhood" #7, #8, and #18 appeared in BMP Voices.

"postcards from the museum of childhood" #6, #10, and #11 appeared in Mom Egg Review.

"@ChazenArtUW the day after a woman loses the presidency like a heart balloon ripped from her fist" appeared in *Undocumented: Great Lakes Poets Laureate on Social Justice* (Michigan State University Press).

"[Some] Facts About the Moon" and "colophon" were originally part of an artist book created for the 2020–21 Arts & Literature Laboratory exhibit "46 Artists for America's First Ladies," Madison, Wisconsin.

Copyright © 2025 by Wendy Vardaman.
All rights reserved.

Published in the United States by Brain Mill Press.
Print ISBN 978-1-948559-92-8
EPUB ISBN 978-1-948559-93-5
Cover art "Targets" by Wendy Vardaman © Wendy Vardaman, 2025.

www.brainmillpress.com

For my mother, Lorna Nelle Grossman Vardaman (1937-2023),
who worked harder than anyone I've known to navigate the maze

contents

piecework	1
postcards from the museum of childhood	
#1	7
#2	8
#3	9
#4	10
#5	11
#6	12
#7	13
#8	14
#9	15
#10	16
#11	17
#12	18
#13	19
#14	20
#15	21
#16	22
#17	23
#18	24
@ChazenArtUW the day after a woman loses the presidency like a heart balloon ripped from her fist	25
[Some] Facts About the Moon	28
colophon	36
about the author	39

thread me an exit

piecework

pasiphaë rocks her infant
    on her lap like any mother.
        hush, little minotaur,
you are no monster. shh. no more
    than any other child & less
        than theseus who left
ariadne on rock outcrop after she
    gifted him with thread
        to navigate / amaze

##

we were on pins and needles that winter. we were on bobby pins. we were on pens and pencils. we were on pincers which could hurt when they caught you by the skin of your teeth then wouldn't let go. we were on pinking shears and pink slips and pink hats. we were on pentagrams and instagrams and pentagons. we were on adapin. but we were not on pentimento. we promised ourselves that much. we would *never* be on pentimento

##

discuss: picasso's representation of women. girls. marie-thérèse. normalization. aestheticization of violence against women. this in a week following the suicide of another. she too had a face that looks good splashed across social. see her in profile. teenage girl her classmates saw as europa. watched under weight of minotaur. bull-man hiding behind bull-mask

##

spin: to draw out. twist fiber into yarn or thread. to form thread. to revolve rapidly. to move swiftly. to set rotating. quantum character of sparticle

twist: to unite by winding. to mingle. to wring wrench dislocate. to distort. to pull off by torsion. to form into spiral. to cause turning. to follow a winding course changing shape. to writhe. act of turning. curve. bend. unexpected occurrence. as in plot. formed by twisting. thread. sewing silk. piece of dough. tobacco leaves. strip of citrus. a dance. spin given to ball. spiral turn. torque applied to body. strain. distortion of meaning. device. trick. front or back dive. eccentricity

##

i dream in monster. edge of house & human. cut my finger on its paper-thin blade. in battle of giant arthropod. oblivious to cataclysmic comedy. the room where we used to sit and read. what did we call it. floored with rot & prairie grass pushing up powder. there were barricades between us & them. there were traps. the signs said keep an eye on the children

##

the signs said keep an eye on the children. the signs said stay inside. stay calm. alert. the signs said not to approach the glass. but you keep peering into death even after i put up blackout curtains. i could always sew anything. i will so us a way out of this poem as soon as i hem the him of human. miter the seems of mother. we think something is out there. it might not matter. i might be sewing with disappearing

##

monitaur the threads of you lead places we don't want to follow. following lines of pvc. of pharmacology. of dextrose & fentanyl & vicodin. amaze me. bully me whole human. thread me an exit. lead us a home. no going path. make me a way. body me back

##

threading the distance between us threading the windows threading the bicycle poised not midair you can see as the lights come up not house lights not hospital not helicopter but the god lights lighting up one more on this less than inevitable this maybe not so only so lonely s h e

##

monster talked to monitor & monitaur replied & momster listened & monitor became monister & monster became moniter & mon(i)(s)ter put away their différance & became
         the   space   between   them

##

& you know this is how you know what you don't know. this finding the godlight. this belief this circle something. these blades that catch find require you to marry monster to monitor. so shadow shivers. so you prepare. so you sew ready

##

it was winter & orfeo
if he always looks back to check
his chain traffic angular momentum
will he sentence me then

i will write that sentence myself
ride it & right it until I re-member

the turn the name this piece
      re-member to flute
           it was winter monitor
it was momitaur

postcards from the museum of childhood

#1

last day of unschool (aka rowing)
for the son, 18,
& when he gets home shirtless
for the Mom-Dad snap, he flexes
his abs, gives the camera some swol—
seersucker seam puckering
his mid-line six months post-op,
though it's tidy, well-made

#2

countdown to college
for the youngest of three.
we make a shortlist of stuff
he can't live without. joke about
what to call us now. joke about where
to find free condoms at Catholic
school. joke about how he stops going
to Mass. joke about SparkNotes, the
Honors Edition. joke about the nth refinance
& who gets the bill. joke about coming
home in case of mental illness breakdown
suicidal ideation. do not decline
health insurance

#3

Skyped the 20-somethings this weekend—
#1 finished a physics master's six months ago.
doesn't know what now.
#2 studies theater. graduates in June.
we get ready to launch #3 without
any knowledge of dynamics
or differential equations. cross our
fingers. wish on lucky stars
that the landing gear locks.
the GPS kicks in

#4

my mom emails to say it's diabetic
neuropathy. which means
what we already know. her foot
doesn't work anymore. they're
making a brace. tell her to use a cane.
she lives in a four-story house. no
ground-floor bathroom. long walk
to the car. the front seat stuck
at his leg length since Dad died five
years ago. they can't fix that either

5

third physical therapy appointment—
hip that brought me already unkinked. back
of the body jaw to ankle still twisted floss.
have you had some extra stress this year?
do a quick inventory. as of this morning
all three kids alive

#6

my neighbor learns to mow
her yard. waves at us from done
from see from learn new things
in retirement. sweeps her arm & smiles.
it's a little shorter than her husband
would have liked. a little shorn.
he's been gone three months.
I miss his *hello, beautiful day,*
daily slow walk around the block
when I think of him, which
isn't often. she seems okay

#7

she's so mother. so mid-life. so mid-
sentence balance & interrupt. so
juggle so long. every thought
toss toss dis-
connect. let alone words.
when the balls blades breakables
stop dropping she doesn't
can't never. what to do with the hands—
so open. so umbrella

#8

Kandinsky at the Milwaukee Art Museum—
fluid shorthand, iconographic lines,
portable symbol kit that packs
at a moment's notice. not fleeing. not holding
on. but strolling unarmed unharmed
through 40 years of politic. of risk.
St. Petersburg–Berlin–Moscow–Weimar–
Berlin–Occupied Paris. bag filled with
the essentials. curic & oars. barbed
wire fence. dragon. spear of Saint George

#9

maybe I don't have a postcard in me today. maybe that's Ferguson. maybe Mike Brown. maybe Robin Williams. maybe Gaza. Iraq. Ukraine. maybe primaries this week. next fall's election. maybe it's 51 & tired. upcoming trips. the drop off. the pick up. youngest leaving for college 800 miles from home. oldest returning 2200 miles. no idea what's next

#10

we grope our way forward. worry
about fall & fall off this flat.
there is black ice at the border
of fine & we keep sliding. there
is fog. you can't see your
feet let alone. you hope
to find your way back some.
not to *happy* which never. but
to *well.* to *well enough.* to get
there you have to understand
what it is to be *there.* you have to
be there. you have to *are* there.
& twist every word in half
break crack this world open
between your teeth. it is tense at the edge
of *okay*. you may have to go on alone

#11

there were things to tell you but
physical therapy. cleaning the fridge.
cat litter. there were meals to make
& messages. if you stop folding
clothes. stop alphabetizing
cabinets & childhood. but there
still isn't enough. there were idioms
to learn. culture. I did not want to
say the things I wanted to say
in the language I had to say them.
but *mother* is the only tongue I know
& when the calendar says *jump*—
I say where. I say when

#12

on the last day before third child goes to college
I get up after a few hours tossing. visions of illness
ER trips regattas recitals communion
confirmation. knowing that I missed
my chance. that independence the older two
had to negotiate & all you had to do was be pleasant.
if I'd thought it would come to this I'd never

#13

husband to the right. 18-year-old behind.
slept fine last night. three well-packed bags
in the living room waiting for lift off.
leisurely dinner kitchen clean-up trash litter.
hem one last shirt. laundry. even leave
the pet sitter a note. *sorry fridge so messy.*
taxi two minutes ahead of schedule.
making a deposit?   we skip a beat.
      get good grades

#14

my mother-in-law clips along at the helm
of her red walker, sails the perimeter.
it's a breeze. does she even need it to steady
her gait? someone has decked her
top to toe in white. white suit, white shirt,
white cotton socks, white sandals—the safe kind
with two buckles on each shoe.
her face powdered white too. two
pink china doll circles where cheeks
go. pink cupid's bow. she knows
my husband is her son—whatever
that means. tells me across
confusion *I can't hear a thing*

#15

Andrew & the Leeches, Daniela Edburg. *Bright Matter,* Shinique Smith. another Chihuly—*Lime Green Icicle Tower.* whatever. Gugger Petter, *Weaving with Newspaper.* Maria Auxiliadora da Silva, *Rain Over São Paulo.* paint strokes designed to look like cross-stitch

#16

when the plane takes off over
the harbor, I realize we haven't
even been down to the water.
white sails stretch to some horizon
or another. the plane rolls
& banks Midwest. toward Chicago.
toward Madison. no one waiting

#17

it's been fun. but honest—I'm tired
of writing in rectangle. in covered
window. in lines of insect making
their way across sticks some kid laid
across a puddle. in lines of children
getting ready to start again day after
Labor Day. in lines of childhood.
maybe these lines will never be bridges
to anywhere anyone. no matter how small

18

the museum of childhood. free admission.
gallery talks by appointment. free recorded
tours. collection highlights for short visits—
theatrical T-shirts & character photos. kindergarten
bird drawings. high school ceramics. legos.
18 porcelain birthday girls (#3 missing
their head). wooden trains—possible lead hazard.
middle school acrylics. class watercolor acquired at auction.
piano cello oboe ice skates cross-country skis.
stuffed animals & dolls. baby blankets. crib bedding.
photo & document collections (e.g. test scores
school projects). hand-knit sweaters. not all items on display

@ChazenArtUW the day after a woman loses the presidency like a heart balloon ripped from her fist

For the master's tools will never dismantle the master's house.
                                                —Audre Lorde
My lord, as I was sewing in my closet
                                        —Ophelia to Polonius

my mother twisted coat hanger into shape then basted
a ruffled ring of stiff net to its wire. insisted
on making a valentine's box I might or might not have made
myself after she got home from work. my dad may or may
not have been reciting *Hamlet* lines to a mirror
at his elbow my brother most certainly watching tv.

my lord as I was sewing in my closet, measuring wire to thread
the needle of your need, feeling sew so, knot knowing what you
    felt.
knot knowing who/what. my ayes began to go. knot sew sharp
    as they were wants.
missing the whole. missing you. dropping stitch after stitch.
turning the hoop. looping together what split in two.
tough muscle so hard to pierce. to draw twist through.

writing your name in blood on skin.
words. words. words. words. words.

##

maybe O sews her own heart
back together in the closet. maybe Gertrude
shows her how some afternoon. *cross stitch with care—*
back/forth down/up over/through
no need to look. so
many tasks that women do seam
like that. the hand keeps an eye on somebody
while the ear watches someone

who doesn't watch back. you don't connect with other
people. *back. forth.* you never have. *down.*
up. this is an overdue valentine
for my mother. *over.*
through. whose Wards store placed clothing orders for Hillary
in Arkansas c. 1972. *back. forth.* who didn't connect to you.

##

while I pried my father's hands off aluminum cans & glass more
   than won
knight to send him to sleep. know matter. my mother still made
   the valentine's box
with a ruffle-wired heart, *Hamlet* scratched across her chest—

to be or not to be twisted like copper around & through
tissue & artery to hold it there. & scratch again when it
   disappeared.
Hamlet. we wrote. & wrote. & wrote. & wrote.

we've been chipping against his shine with pens & needles
when glass can be spun. woven. knit. crimped. bent.

wake up, sweet ladies. Hamlet's cracked mirror is not for you.

yours knot for hem.

if I have to cut you out of my art, then mend
it once an hour, I will. if I have to make this the last word I type

& poem in sewn paper. in rickrack & button. in wrinkle
& torn. in silkscreen & pressure. in saddle-stitch & barbed wire
   net

[Some] Facts About the Moon

> *Now I was a symbol—and that was a new experience.*
> —Hillary Diane Rodham Clinton 2004

[subject to change]

moonshine
promise the moon
honeymoon
moon mission
many moons ago
shoot for the moon
moon rock
moon launch
once in a blue moon
over the moon
moon over
reach for the moon
moon dust
ask for the moon

1. About Arrows

> *We arrived not knowing what was possible. Consequently, we expected a lot. We found that there was a gap between expectation and reality.* HDRC 1969

Diana
Patron of the countryside
Patron of hunters of crossroads
Patron of the moon

There was a girl who emerged from an unchipped, white China cup. One of a set of 12. She waited for the other 11 goddesses to join her.

When they did not, she stepped out of the cold cup of weak tea with its perfect round saucer, removed a full sash of Girl Scout badges, slung the arrows she'd collected so far onto her back, and went into the world wearing thick, rose-colored glasses.

who's a good girl
hit like a girl
run like a girl
cry like a girl
big-girl pants
big girls don't cry
cover girl
girl Friday
Goldwater girl
girls who wear glasses
glamour girl
call girl
little girls' room
girl next door
working girl

2. Outdoor Voices

> *I suppose I could have stayed home and baked cookies and had teas, but what I decided to do was to fulfill my profession.* HDRC 1992

> *Equated with Artemis*
> *Virgin goddess*
> *Goddess of childbirth*
> *Advice giver*
> *Finder of lost objects*
> *Twin to Apollo*
> *Midwife to Apollo*

She carried her makeshift porcelain quiver of arrows everywhere. She kept her eye out for a bow. She kept her eye on the moon.

One fine, yellow morning, she discovered a perfect moon-faced baby in a little teacup & raised her. She strapped on this cup, too, and carried it a long, long way. One more, it seemed, was exactly enough.

extra kleenex
sunglasses
snow pants
pen & notebook
sunscreen
bandaids
scotch tape

crayons
glue
scissors
glitter
flashlight
reflective vest
stop sign
whistle
cards
snacks
megaphone
needle & thread
extra buttons
comb
scrunchies
masks

3. Crossing Guards

> *The truth is that sometimes it is hard even for me to recognize the Hillary Clinton that other people see.* HDRC 1995

> *Goddess of crossroads*
> *Patron of families*
> *House breaker*
> *Bringer of curses & plague*
> *Bringer of plenty*

She adjusted her hair. She changed costumes. She tried on different accents wandering place to place.

Everything that she wanted to do took SOOOOOOO much time & she was running out of time to save the world.

Sometimes she made friends and sometimes enemies.

exceptionalism
containment
border security
interventionism
deterrence
pragmatism
détente
mutual defense
regional trade block
globalization

War on Terror
collective defense
New World Order
neocolonialism
multilateralism
doctrine of enlargement

4. About Eros

I believe in redemption, I guess. HDRC 2020

> *Married to Lucifer*
> *Mother of a daughter*
> *Archer hunter healer*
> *Triple deity—merged with the moon & underworld*
> *Goddess of wilderness*

Eventually, she said loudly to herself what she had only just learned: that humans are fickle & unpredictable, even though the world is round & has a countable number of people & countries in it with more or less the same set of complex problems to solve—
    In a different world, she might have shot the moon—

in a different world she might have never aimed an arrow—

was it not enough
    to be the fletcher,
      to gather the feathers,
    to craft their shaft
to define its spine?

                                          fletching
                                              nock
                                              shaft
                                              spine
                                        anchor point

target panic
broadheads
blunts
points
quiver
bullseye
bracing
overdrawn
flex
quarrel
string
draw
cap tang
sinew
hafting
ferrule
fletcher
release

colophon

the gates were hard and so were the gatekeepers. we did the best we could & sometimes we tried to hurry things up. we threw ourselves at glass doors & glass ceilings. glass railings & glass elevators & skylights. sometimes we lay down on the hard glass floors & pummeled them & cried a river of glass. we lived in glass houses & our eyes got glassy watching tvs & pcs & zoom rooms & children. we spun glass & wove it & wound it into balls of glass thread that unraveled behind us on the way to where we thought we were going. we tried to do what we wanted & we left others behind. when we got there & were turned away because we weren't good enough or just *NO* some of us kept trying & some of us gave up. it was hard work trying to human. we mistook our daughters for partners & friends when they were on their own journeys. sometimes we wrote off our husbands/fathers/sons. sometimes they wrote us off. we got mad at our mothers & then we took care of them dying as best we could & felt sad. we got jobs & tried to pay the bills. we tried to save for the long stretch when our partners & family & friends were gone. we were lonely starting out then busy then lonely again. lonelybusylonelybusylonelybusylonely. we were stuck in a maze we didn't make & couldn't find a way out. we looked for cracks. we looked for gaps. it was clear. you could see right through the glass

about the author

Wendy Vardaman (wendyvardaman.com), PhD, works as a web and digital media specialist. She is the author of *Obstructed View* (2009), *Reliquary of Debt* (2015), and the chapbook (with Sarah Sadie) *Rules of (dis)engagement, or Dubious perFormances* (2016). In addition to poetry, her creative practice includes editing, prose writing, illustration, printmaking, and design. One of two Madison, Wisconsin, poets laureate from 2012 to 2015, she currently volunteers as a graphic designer for poetry projects. She received the 2024 Dick Scuglik Memorial Fellowship and residency for writing about art at Write On, Door County and a 2025 residency at Ragdale.

www.ingramcontent.com/pod-product-compliance
Lightning Source LLC
Chambersburg PA
CBHW052127070526
44586CB00016B/2114